Pebble® Plus

Whale Sharks

by Deborah Nuzzolo

CAPSTONE PRESS
a capstone imprint

Pebble Plus is published by Capstone Press,
1710 Roe Crest Drive, North Mankato, Minnesota 56003
www.mycapstone.com

Library of Congress Cataloging-in-Publication Data
Names: Nuzzolo, Deborah, author.
Title: Whale sharks / by Deborah Nuzzolo.
Description: North Mankato, Minnesota : Capstone Press, [2017] | Series:
Pebble plus. All about sharks | Audience: Ages 4–8. | Audience: K to grade 3. |
Includes bibliographical references and index.
Identifiers: LCCN 2016059069| ISBN 9781515769996 (library binding) |
ISBN 9781515770053 (pbk.) | ISBN 9781515770114 (ebook (pdf))
Subjects: LCSH: Whale shark—Juvenile literature. | CYAC: Sharks.
Classification: LCC QL638.95.R4 B35 2018 | DDC 597.3/3—dc23
LC record available at https://lccn.loc.gov/2016059069

Editorial Credits
Nikki Bruno Clapper, editor; Kayla Rossow, designer;
Kelly Garvin, media researcher; Gene Bentdahl, production specialist

Photo Credits
Minden Pictures: Peter Verhoog/Buiten-beeld, 17, Reinhard Dirscheri, 13; Shutterstock: belizediversity,
1, divedog, 24, Dudarev Mikhail, 15, kaschibo, 9, kataleewan intarachote, 2, Krzysztof Odziomek,
cover, 5, Rich Carey, 21, SeraphP, 19, Thanakon S, 7, Willyam Bradberry, 23; Superstock/FLPA, 11

Artistic elements
Shutterstock: Apostrophe, HorenkO, Magenta10

Note to Parents and Teachers

The All About Sharks set supports national curriculum standards for science
related to the characteristics and behavior of animals. This book describes and
illustrates whale sharks. The images support early readers in understanding the
text. The repetition of words and phrases helps early readers learn new words.
This book also introduces early readers to subject-specific vocabulary words,
which are defined in the Glossary section. Early readers may need assistance to
read some words and to use the Table of Contents, Glossary, Read More, Internet
Sites, Critical Thinking Questions, and Index sections of the book.

Printed in China.
004704

Table of Contents

Giant of the Sea

A huge shark swims

slowly in the sea.

It opens its wide mouth.

It pulls in tiny sea animals.

This is a whale shark.

Whale sharks are
the world's largest fish.
They live in warm seas.
These gentle giants are
not dangerous to people.

Lots of Spots

Whale sharks have a long body and a wide, flat head. The mouth can be 5 feet (1.5 meters) wide.

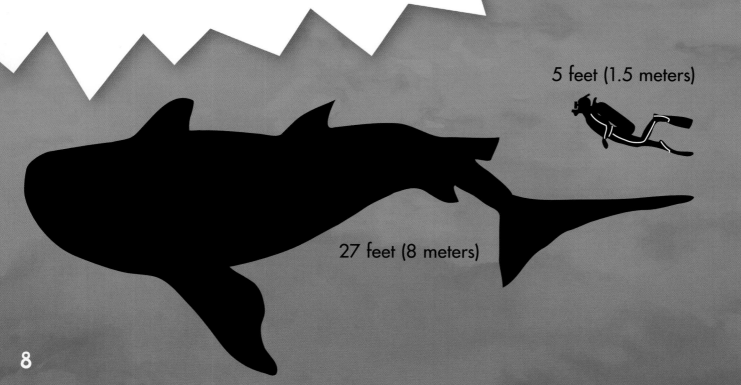

5 feet (1.5 meters)

27 feet (8 meters)

A whale shark is gray
with a white belly.
It has lots of spots.
Its eyes are small.

The skeleton of a

whale shark bends easily.

It is made of cartilage.

Cartilage is softer than bone.

Eating

Whale sharks are big,
but their food is small.
They eat tiny plants and
animals called plankton.
They also eat fish and squid.

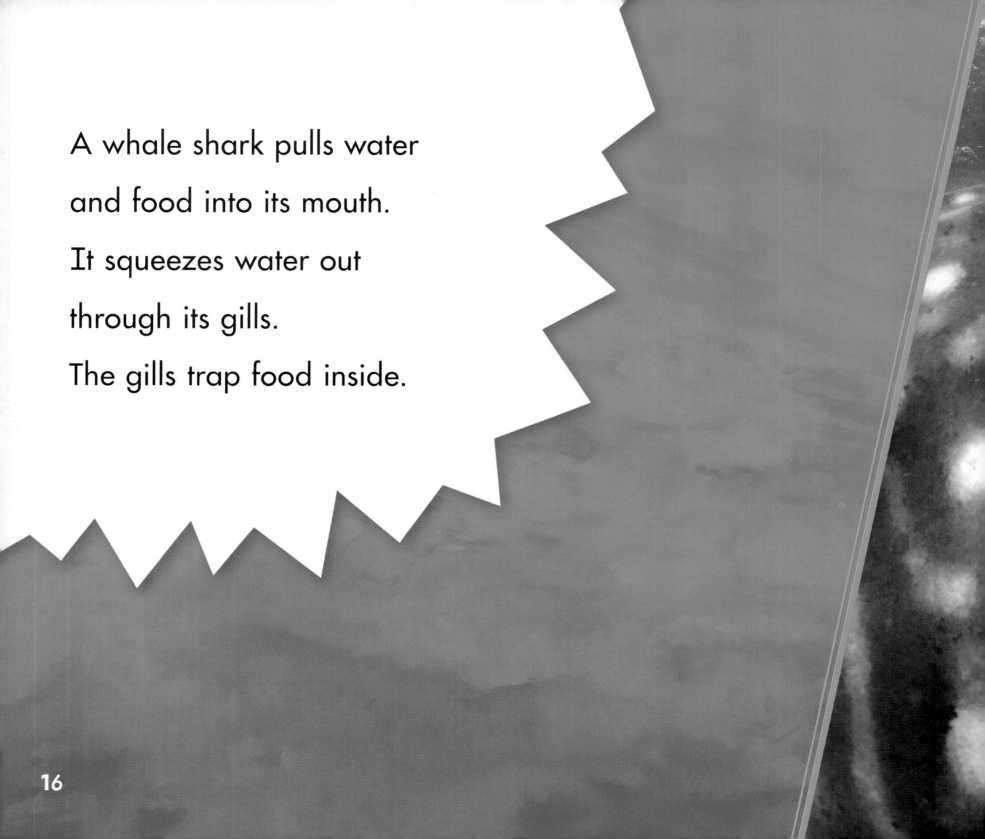

A whale shark pulls water
and food into its mouth.
It squeezes water out
through its gills.
The gills trap food inside.

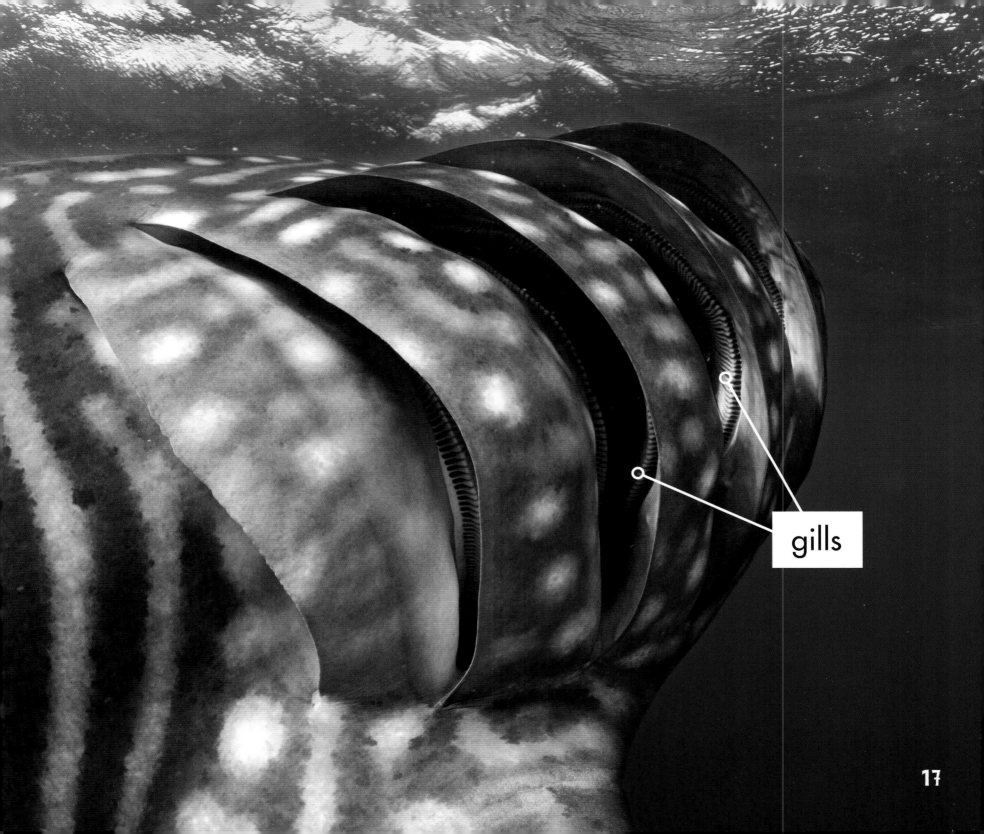

gills

Whale Shark Babies

Whale shark pups hatch from eggs inside their mother. Up to 300 pups are born at one time.

The pups are more than
2 feet (61 centimeters) long.
They live on their own.
Whale sharks live
for 70 years or longer.

Glossary

cartilage—the strong, bendable material that forms some body parts on humans and other animals

dangerous—likely to cause harm or injury

gentle—kind and calm

gill—a body part on the side of a fish; fish use their gills to breathe

hatch—to break out of an egg

plankton—tiny plants and animals that drift in the sea

pup—a young shark

skeleton—the bones that support and protect the body of a human or other animal

squid—a sea animal with a long, soft body and 10 fingerlike arms used to grasp food

Read More

Hanson, Anders. *Whale Shark.* Giant Animals. North Mankato, Minn.: ABDO Publishing Company, 2014.

McAneney, Caitie. *In Search of Whale Sharks.* Shark Search. New York: PowerKids Press, 2016.

Susumu, Shingu. *Wandering Whale Sharks.* Berkeley, Calif.: Owlkids Books, Inc., 2015.

Internet Sites

FactHound offers a safe, fun way to find Internet sites related to this book. All of the sites on FactHound have been researched by our staff.

Here's all you do:

Visit *www.facthound.com*

Type in this code: 9781515769996

 Check out projects, games and lots more at **www.capstonekids.com**

Critical Thinking Questions

1. How do whale sharks eat?

2. What is cartilage? How does cartilage help whale sharks move?

3. What do you think it would be like to swim with a whale shark?

Index